JOURNEY
to the
LOST CITY

Jonathan Aaron

AUSABLE PRESS
2006

Design and composition by Ausable Press
The type is Perpetua with Perpetua Titling.
Cover design by Rebecca Soderholm

Published by
Ausable Press
1026 Hurricane Road
Keene, NY 12942
www.ausablepress.org

Distributed to the trade by
Consortium Book Sales & Distribution
1045 Westgate Drive
Saint Paul, MN 55114-1065
(651) 221-9035
(651) 221-0124 (fax)
(800) 283-3572 (orders)

Library of Congress Cataloging-in-Publication Data

Aaron, Jonathan
Journey to the lost city / Jonathan Aaron. —1st ed.
p. cm.
Includes bibliographical references.
ISBN 1-931337-30-6 (pbk. : alk. paper)
1. Title
PS3551.A7J68 2006
811'.54–dc22
2006034202

for Lawrence Raab

CONTENTS

This Little System

as evening began to fall a dog barked
but why did I think he's barking as if
he knows we are not coming back
　　　　　　　—Rutger Kopland

THIS LITTLE SYSTEM

of branchy twigs a few dead leaves
still cling to, along with three or four
shreds of sun-stiffened paper, a bit of string,
occasionally a weather-faded ribbon, feels

prickly, oddly solid, yet ready to float
from your hand. Lidded—roofed—it might be
a box or a tiny house meant for nothing
bigger than a bird or a mouse. Don't ask me

why at night it emits a fitful glow,
abrupt flashes, periodic spokes of light.
What do I know? Someone inside's up late

reading, or snooping with a flashlight. Or signalling
that long, low, darkened ship lying in
close to shore, doubtless up to no good.

1

EXPLETIVES

Words that leap unexpectedly to my lips,
you steer me clear of my nostalgia for civility
and my sorry habit of rummaging
in the works of big-time philosophers for aphorisms
that might elevate my soul.
You don't give a rat's ass for my secret wish to at least once
in my life quote Montaigne exactly.
At the slightest whiff of semantics you scurry
for the total darkness just beyond moments from now, where you hide
in the tuneless singing of everything
that hasn't happened yet.
But I've always been certain of you—
how quickly you pointed out
the difference between the onion
I thought I was chopping
and the suddenly bloody head of my left thumb,
the face in the window
and the backlit leaves flinching in the wind.
And when the end of autumn came to me
on the first day of spring, you steadied my stagger.
When I glimpsed through flailing wipers
those three rain-flung
birds spinning for an instant
above oncoming traffic, you spoke
my mind before I knew what it was. And this morning,
when I saw the front page of the *New York Times,* you were waiting
and ready for me, right
on the money, words, little words, the very last
I heard my mother say.

THE END OF *OUT OF THE PAST*

(RKO Pictures, 1947)

"I never told you I was anything but what I am," she says.
Black and white, the sunset behind Lake Tahoe looks spectacular.
She turns and goes upstairs, his chance to light a cigarette
and dial the operator. She slips the pistol into her briefcase,
gives the bathroom a cursory final glance. Moments later,
sitting on the couch, he hands her a shot of brandy.
"Thanks," she says. *"Por nada,"* he answers, pouring one
for himself. She says she thinks they both deserve a break. "We deserve
each other," he replies, and wings his glass into the empty fireplace.
She's unperturbed, strictly business, already in Mexico.
His sleepy expression shows he knows exactly where they're going.
Night has already covered most of the country. The airwaves
are vibrating with the strains of "Sentimental Journey," "Satin Doll,"
and "String of Pearls." As they get into his Chevy station wagon,
I could be five and just waking up from another nightmare.
Half the world is lying in ruins.

SOME THOUGHTS ABOUT
WORLD WAR II AIRPLANES

1

Named for real and imaginary birds, beasts, and insects,
weather phenomena and difficult emotions,
their cowling air-scoops slightly loony grins,
they looked dog-tame and lethal at the same time.
Last night on the History Channel I saw them lining up
at the end of a desert runway in a waver of heat,
then taking off in a whiteout on the Russian Front.

American air crews decorated the noses of their planes
with pet names ("Miss Mary Lou," "Calamity Jane"),
wisecracks ("Grin-'N-Bear-It," "What-U-Need"),
and cartoons—an angry Donald Duck with his dukes up,
a girl-devil in high heels and nothing else,
a skull and crossbones settling back
after another day of work, reading a book.

2

Summers when I was a kid, my grandfather
would take me to his favorite hardware store
and buy me a balsa glider. I'd shake the feathery
sections from the paper sleeve and check the wing
by holding it up to the light, the delicate fuselage,

tail pieces the size and weight of potato chips.
I'd cautiously ease the wing through its splintery slot,
then work the metal weight onto the nose.
The tail fin often fell off as I got ready to throw.

His two sons served in the Navy during the war,
one in the Aleutians, the other on the carrier *Randolph*
in the Philippine Sea. He swore—and I think he meant what he said—
that if either were killed he would go down to Washington
and personally assassinate President Roosevelt.

3
A rich insurance broker who never paid his taxes,
impulsive, piratical, he felt comfortable behind the wheel
of a big car and didn't believe in speed limits.
One evening, heading home from Boston
in his Lincoln convertible, he had a heart attack,
but he managed to stay alive long enough
to pull over and turn off the engine.

The lawn in back of his summer house
stretched to a low stone wall at the edge of a bluff
that dropped sharply to the beach along the Canal.
The pale, stiff grass it hurt to walk on barefoot
turned blue as the sun went down and the revolving flash
of the lighthouse grew brighter and brighter, looking into my mind.
The flagpole lanyard clanged all night in the wind.

A LESSON

for John Willett

Maybe the School Board had decided that attending
Miss Halloran's funeral would be educational.
There we were, the entire fourth grade, fidgeting

in the high-backed, uncushioned pews of Saint Mary's.
I watched my breath appear and disappear in the cold air.
Who of us, I wondered, had already seen a dead person?

The priest started talking. His voice seemed to come
from the shadows that troubled me whenever
I looked up. It sounded familiar, like someone

from *Sky King,* or *True Detective Mysteries.*
Miss Halloran was with the angels now,
it said. And so were all those American and South

Korean boys. Each day, they rose
from rise paddies and snowy mountainsides
into the healing safety of the sky, body and soul

restored to wholeness thanks to a power far,
far stronger than a mother's love. While North Korean and Chinese
soldiers—human waves—kept pouring into a fiery abyss,

to burn alive forever at the planet's core.
If we really listened, we could hear it happening.
If we closed our eyes, we could see it for ourselves.

And here he paused, daring us not to.

A NIGHT IN SPOLETO

Talk ranged from the latest arrested senator,
to the bizarre stigmata of a local
saint, to how very sweet today's tomatoes tasted
in olive oil, lemon juice, and lots of fresh basil.

The wine and trying to understand Italian
made the room tilt—time, I thought, to search
out the library. Finding it dark,
I felt the wall for a light switch.

Five bulbs thinly disguised as candle flames appeared
to waver near the ceiling, not shedding much light
on what took shape of the nineteenth century.
Two fat sofas and an easy chair, cheek-by-jowl, tight-

lipped, pressurized, like feuding relations
listening to a will being read. Tarnished mirrors
on either side of a mantelpiece, each posing as a window
wiped with a dirty sleeve for a better look at the interior.

The portrait of a woman in a brown silk dress sitting
at a piano, hands lifted, waiting to begin,
faced the portrait of a man gesturing proudly
at a landscape on fire beyond a half-drawn curtain.

As she flexed her fingers above the keyboard, drawing his glance,
voices rose and footsteps came and went
in a rush down the hallway behind me, and door after
door started slamming in what had to be the wind.

ANXIOUS DREAMS

How lucky I am tonight to be holding a lantern
at this railroad crossing in the middle of America
and not clinging to a leaky raft on the north Atlantic,
or plunging from a cliff in Nepal because my rope broke.
As the lights and noise of the train wane and die out,

I can hear my wife snoring into her pillow
and the dogs on either side of our bed snoring
into theirs. What was it I was doing a moment ago?
That's it: trying to remember the name of the actor
who played the Lone Ranger on the radio.

The Lone Ranger on the radio always sounded as if he had a cold.
Clayton Moore played the role on television. I hope Clayton
Moore and Jay Silverheels as Tonto, the Lone Ranger's faithful
Indian companion, were friends in real life. Or at least
that they more than just respected each other.

Whoa, there. Steady, big fellow, the masked man would say
reassuringly to his horse Silver, who spooked sometimes,
then always calmed at the sound of his master's voice...
A sudden beam of light through a hole in the clouds
silhouettes a hovering bird of prey. It occurs to me

that Tonto's hardy pinto and Silver are like
Gunnar Björnstrand's squire and Max Von Sydow's knight
in Bergman's early film, *The Seventh Seal.*
I'm in the middle of the fourteenth-century,
having just stepped onto Swedish soil

after twenty wasted years in the Holy Land.
Soon a third of Europe's population will die of the Plague.
Our crusade was so stupid, the squire tells me,
that only an idealist could have thought of it.
The knight is staring intently at the palm of his hand,

his pulse quickening at the prospect of playing chess
with Death. One moment I'm standing beside them,
the next I'm all alone on the crest of a steep dune
overlooking a dim prospect of the Baltic. Far below, two horses
are walking fetlock-deep in the foaming shallows.

Knight and squire lie motionless on the sand, where hunger
and exhaustion must have dropped them into anxious dreams.
Two more horses amble into view, a white Arabian followed by
a stocky paint. The four of them touch noses, nod to each other,
and lower their heads to the nervous, undrinkable water.

LINGERING EFFECTS OF THE SOVIET ERA

Leafing through *Russia in the 20th Century:*
A Photographic History, I find a two-page spread showing Stalin
smiling and a gigantic hand throwing a switch
just like the one in Dr. Frankenstein's laboratory.
And what if I'd actually been involved in this panoramic
view of Magnetogorsk, a city named for a small generator
of alternating current with permanent magnets, used
in the ignition systems of some internal combustion engines?
I doubt I could've lasted even an hour.

You're standing at the stove tending a risotto *alla Milanese,*
its almost palpable amalgam of aromas, of flavors,
its molten unguency, the little kissing sounds it makes
nearing perfection in the heavy pot. You pour more broth
and continue stirring, then pause to observe,
"Buster Keaton survived three train wrecks and five hotel fires,
had no formal schooling, was constantly engaged
in a fatalistic struggle with the mechanical world,
and said he got his best ideas in the bathroom."

A single bulb glows over the kitchen table.
Two white bowls and the spoons beside them shine
in the would-be darkness like a still life by what's-his-name.
"Let's eat," you say, but scratchy music from the public
address system draws me to the window.
The park's floodlit pines look freshly dusted with snow.
All those couples in rowboats drifting out on the lake,
everyone holding up their hands—are they demonstrating
they don't really need their oars, or are they surrendering?

THE SUPERNATURAL

I'm ten years old. No pair of words
can outclass "flying buttress."
Any belfrey has to have bats in it.
A full moon always signifies the weird.

But I don't like entering the attic by myself.
And down in the cellar, past the soapstone sink,
a deeper, denser darkness warns me
to mind my own business.

One summer night on the beach Paul Chavchevadze
puts aside his guitar and tells us kids
about what he saw just before leaving
for North Africa back in 1942.

(Paul is "a Georgian prince," but we don't know
what that means. Nina, his wife, is "a Romanov."
We don't know what that means, either.)
He's saying,

. . . I woke up at 3 a.m.
to the sound of wind in the leaves
and hoofbeats coming and going
around the house. The noises died away.

A woman appeared in the doorway.
What's the matter? I asked.
I thought it was my hostess,
but it wasn't. Very quietly

she crossed the room to my bed.
Despite the dark, I could see
her eyes were green.
You have a dead friend in the next room,

she said with great satisfaction.
I learned in the morning
she had been making such appearances
for nearly two hundred years.

And as she always told the truth,
the one she was referring to, my friend,
a fellow officer, died of a fever
in Egypt six months later.

The surf rears and thumps
in the shadows behind him.
The firelight makes him look like different people
from one moment to the next.

DISAPPEARANCES

Your first pocketknife, that speckled stone
the ocean smoothed, a hand-carved ivory button—
do such things vanish in a blue flash that leaves
a trace of ozone? In a momentary whisper,

as of silk on skin or wind in the leaves?
Weightless in the privacy of being
unobserved, do they rise toward a door
in the air that sighs as it opens and closes?

Water trembles in a glass—it can hardly wait
to achieve the status of a cloud. The edges of an object
look like blurred horizons when all those molecules
start revving their tiny engines, preparing

to take off for that dimension where anything
anyone ever lost is to be found—*lost*
to us meaning *found* to the item itself.
Think about it. As you read these words,

a million sewing needles are flying out of this world
like drops of water haloing a dog shaking herself
after a dip in the ocean. Along with teaspoons,
wedding rings, little pieces of paper with numbers on them,

half of almost any pair of socks. And not just
tables and chairs: the contents of entire houses,
the houses themselves, cruise ships full of giddy vacationers,
small towns, the occasional city—disappearances

requiring only that the rest of us be kept completely in the dark.
So much for your fountain pen, your sunglasses,
the only photo of her face how many years ago. So much
for the car keys now almost invisible on the shelf

in the unlit hallway you turn to look back down, remembering
all over again the leaf-strewn homeward path
children in stories since stories began
search for and never recover.

2

OFFSHORE FORECAST

Maybe it started that day off Falmouth when our springer spaniel,
leaning over the bow of my grandfather's motorboat,
started barking at the grey triangular fin that broke the swell
just ahead and then ran upright for a good fifteen seconds
before tilting slowly back into the green,
collective doubt of everyone on board except me and the dog.

Or maybe the day my grandfather stood in his swimming trunks
on the shore of the little harbor he owned, pointing at
a long shadow lazily executing a series of figure-8s
just below the water's surface, each numeral
the width of the inlet. Or maybe, after all, it started
when I read about a famous scuba-diver's repeated

dream: he's off Montauk, a couple of fathoms down, and then
the small fish around him abruptly vanish, signalling
something very big approaching very fast. . . . For whatever reason,
I can't remember when I haven't felt on edge,
a kind of dread, ready for wreck and erasure, whenever I listen
to someone talking seriously about the ocean.

As I do tonight driving home tuned to the weather
station's latest offshore forecast. *Seas of one to two feet,*
a voice is saying through static that makes the words sound
authoritative. *Winds variable, becoming southerly 10
to 15 knots. Seas increasing to 3 and 4 feet by morning.*
I can see a vast stretch of dents and creases,

a restless waste empty of everything
but its own incessant, ravenous expectancy. Daylight's dying
behind me, but I'm low enough over the waves to glimpse
a trawler pitching in the running sea, a gun-camera image
out of a wartime documentary, and after that
what might be the last ray of sun on a sail. And now

I'm underwater, where nothing touches
the serenity of the held breath I agree to
until what's homing in on me becomes
the looming bulk of a truck in the rain
that hammers the windshield, shrouding the oncoming traffic
and the glowing string of pearls in my rearview mirror.

SKILLS

Blondin made a fortune walking back and forth
over Niagara Falls on a tightrope—blindfolded,
or inside a sack, or pushing a wheelbarrow, or perched on stilts,
or lugging a man on his back. Once, halfway across,
he sat down to cook and eat an omelette.

Houdini, dumped into Lake Michigan chained
and locked in a weighted trunk, swam back to the boat
a few moments later. He could swallow more than a hundred needles
and some thread, then pull from between his lips
the needles dangling at even intervals.

I can close my eyes and see your house
explode in a brilliant flash, silently,
with a complete absence of vibration. And when I open them again,
my heart in my mouth, everything is standing
just as before, but not as if nothing had happened.

MR. MOTO'S CONFESSION

The famous Tokyo detective looked as if he'd taken a shower
in his linen suit and then slept in it.
He mopped his shiny forehead with a handkerchief.
"Pascal was right," he said, his tenor slightly nasal.
"Men are so necessarily mad, that not to be mad would amount to
another form of madness. What's more," he added, the cat
eyeing the canary, "contradiction is not a sign of falsity,
nor is the want of contradiction a sign of truth—Pascal again."
He took out his fountain pen. I saw my chance.
"Mr. Moto," I asked, "should I believe all those stories
I've heard about you?" "Please do not," he murmured. "I do not."
He was writing something on a cocktail napkin.
"In fact," he said, his pen continuing to move, "my real name is
Laszlo Löwenstein. I was born in Hungary, I drove myself crazy
as an actor in Zurich and Berlin, and now that I live in Hollywood
I have bad dreams. Last night one of them told me
I'll end up buried alive in a tale by Edgar Allan Poe."
He coughed politely, capped his pen, and getting to his feet
handed me the flimsy patch of paper. "An ancient Japanese
poetic form," he said. Even as I stared at it
the little cairn of characters, each a tiny, exotic bird cage
with its doors open, blurred, melted, and reformed as if rising
to the surface of a well, where these words trembled
but stayed clear enough to read: *As evening nears, how clearly
a dog's bark carries over the water.*

THE WOLF OF GUBBIO

for Anthony Hecht

It was one of those towns with practically no perspective,
the architecture half-geometrical, houses upon houses
stacked at dizzy angles. Clouds the shape and color of laurel leaves
hung in a pale blue sky. The locals walking around wore
guilty looks, conscious, as always, of having something to hide.
Flowers grew in doorways, abundant, untended, extending
themselves in gestures of inquiry and yearning. Iridescent songbirds
plunged through the air, heedless of what might be waiting
in the forest at the foot of mountains that appeared
deliberately jagged. An angel, robed and golden-haired,
floated absent-mindedly above a garden. Farther off
and smaller in scale, a bat-winged devil, whose grimace
augured either laughter or tears, crouched on a rooftop.
A lake, or possibly the sea, gleamed at the distant end of a road
that wound through other towns, each a staid collection of arches
and towers like bunches of white asparagus in the noonday sun.
Saint Francis liked to sing in French and knew the troubadors.
Bending forward, he did not look directly into the eyes of the animal,
who cocked his head, thought for a moment, and started wagging his tail.

FRANK

My big dog Frank has a blue eye
and a brown eye. At fifteen he walks
with difficulty—his back legs seem to work
by afterthought—though he springs to his feet
for the mailman or a UPS truck.

Right now he's asleep.
The pink tip of his tongue pokes
over the black, outfolded ripple of his lower lip.
His narrowed eyes give his almost completely
white face a Kabuki look.

He still loves his supper.
He will not do without his carrot.
He's practically deaf, except for when he thinks
he isn't. After
the vet fixed his larynx, we had to remember his bark.

Dreaming,
he arches his neck and thrusts his four legs forward
as if skidding to a stop. Descartes thought
animals are machines. He couldn't see
that dreaming is after all a kind of thinking.

In a photograph
young Frank sits at the edge of the street,
not looking the camera in the eye,
a beige Toyota Corolla parked just behind him,
its license plate's red letters spelling DOUBT.

Every day these days he's a little bit
sleepier, a little bit more
elsewhere. Once the ground thaws we'll bury
my mother's ashes in a place I still can't find
on a map. Frank scratches the floor,

bares his teeth, licks his lips.
From his throat comes the clicking noise
he makes whenever a dream shows him something
exciting. Still in a trance, he lifts his head and stares, not yet
certain what he sees is what he sees.

ALMA PERDIDA

(after Valery Larbaud)

Yours—vague aspirations, enthusiasms,
after-lunch musings, surges of the heart;
tender lassitude following satisfaction
of the body's needs; strokes of genius; digestion's
agitations when they happen, digestion's contentment
when they're settled; joys for no reason;
the blood's befuddled circulation; recollections of love;
scent of benzoin from the morning's tub; erotic reveries;
my great Castilian foolery, my immense
Puritan despondency, my special weakness for
chocolate, candies so sweet they burn, arctic drinks;
anesthetizing cigars; somniferous cigarettes;
delights of speed, pleasure of sitting still, excellence
of sleep in the utter dark;
juicy news items, noble poetry of the usual; journeys;
gypsies; sleigh rides; rain falling into the sea;
delirium of a fevered night alone with a few books;
highs and lows of weather and temperament;
recurring glimpses of another life; memories, prophecies;
splendors of the beaten path and daily grind—
this lost soul is yours.

VAN GOGH AND THE WIND

He heard it stir in the rosebushes
and flowering oleander crowding the garden of the asylum

in Saint-Rémy, in a "bread-crust"-colored wheatfield extending
as far as a solitary cypress, in staked-out vines that burned in the sun.

He heard it coursing through some weather-broken pines
against a reddish late-afternoon sky, shaking

the yellow leaves of lime trees in the park, fanning the green flames
of olive grove after olive grove, cedars

shading a cedarwalk, a great rhododendron leaning
as if in worry toward faceless, bundled strollers. It sounded like

crickets among the cornstalks lined up at sunset behind a lone reaper,
like voices on the other side of a flowering apple orchard.

It echoed from the hills beyond a landscape with haystacks
and a rising moon, from out of the depths of a gorge called Les Peyroulets.

For a moment he heard it when he put his ear to the white blossoms
of an almond branch standing in a glass of water, and when

his eye fell on the corpse of a little brown bat, which he took back to
his room
and whose wings glowed while he held the animal, with sympathy

and respect, up to the light. Once or twice he thought he heard it
in the big bunches of roses and irises he painted shortly before leaving,

"cured" at last, for the North, where he heard it again,
near Auvers, as curtains of rain swept toward him out of troubled skies,

and behind the calling of the crows that flung themselves
this way and that above the surging wheatfields

he kept returning to, nearing the day he took the pistol
with him, not knowing what he would do

until he got there, leaned his easel against a haystack,
and shot himself just below the heart. During the two days

he took to die, while shadows at his bedside loomed
and subsided and the bright sun in pictures that still came to him

fervently beat down, he listened to it. Then his brother heard him say,
I would like to go like this. And half an hour later he was gone.

THREE HISTORICAL MOMENTS

Innocent III, Father of the Inquisition,
liked to lecture pilgrims on the nature of the Eucharist.
After poking a supplicant in the ribs with his shepherd's crook,
he scanned the sky with his one good eye.
His sign of peace still lingered hours after he disappeared.

Saint Francis could cure lepers, cast out demons, raise the dead.
One day a follower offered him a basket
containing an incredibly lifelike wooden baby.
Take a look at this! the holy mystic whispered,
his outstretched arms sprouting branches for a flock of sparrows.

Though Shakespeare was to represent her as a witch,
Joan of Arc really did hear celestial voices.
Not given to airs, her hair cut short like a soldier's,
she put a finger to her lips so we could listen
to the churchbell tolling somewhere near the edge of town.

NARCISSUS, ECHO

If he'd had an ounce of sense—
but he didn't, he was who he was, destined
for that face looking up at him
from the little forest pool he knelt beside.
"I can't believe it's you," he said, trying to touch
the cheek of the one who had at last, he thought,
drawn near. The watery visage wrinkled, blurred,
then cleared in time for him to glimpse a cloud
changing shape in the sky behind them both. Echo
watched and listened to him pleading with his own
reflection. All she could do was hear herself repeat
the tag-ends of his broken phrases,
the sounds of his crazy laughter and his weeping.
She saw a pallor steal across his features,
a dimness start to cover him like a veil,
and his body suddenly sink into the ground
with the noise of a strangled sigh. Only a little
white flower with a cup-shaped central crown
remained to mark the spot where he had pined
so quickly and completely away.
But though his vanishing happened in a hurry,
in fact it would take him days to get to hell.
When he finally reached its dimly backlit suburbs,
he ran to an embankment on the Styx
in hopes of yet another encounter with
whoever had led him there.
She stayed where she was, already only voice,
never uttering more than the last two syllables
of anything she hears, not because she can't
say more, but because true meaning lies
in sounds we briefly hear a second time.

The birdsong ending a dream of hurried footsteps.
A child's awkward chord on the piano.
And once, as I recall, my own name
from the depths of a limestone quarry,
its waters hoarding a history of junked cars,
unlucky swan-divers, and who knows what other
offerings to the shades and infernal gods.

THE WAY OF THE WORLD

Tiffany goes out and buys a gun after Jack tells her Louise
is more important than material things.

Nadine's heart problem improves at the psychiatric clinic,
but Al's doesn't.

Trying to downplay Amber's uncertainty
about the relation between reason and instinct,
Shannon tells the cops she saw Emily's spirit

wandering around inside Harold's elegant coastal mansion
like she owned the place.

Barbara nixes joining Gabrielle's revenge plot
against Danny because it runs counter to everything
she learned in law school.

After lunch James and Luis agree that Luis's mother
has to get her own lifestyle.

A face in the hallway mirror tells Julian why
Christine's religious fervor can't explain her personal theory
of revelations, but Stacy won't let on

about not being able to carry Kevin's child
(who probably would have been feral, anyhow).

Bix drives out to the Vista del Mar for a longer view of the sea.

Flocks of starlings are conducting their ritual
formation flying over the smoke-filled streets of the city.

The horizon appears on fire in the setting sun.

I'm staring out the kitchen window
as lengthening shadows offer a moment of silence
for what they remind me of,

and I'm thinking the guy could have been right
who said that one day the so-called Dark Ages
will be thought of as including our own.

The next thing you know, it's nearly midnight.

DINNER WITH FERNANDO REY

We pass under the arch of a gate
and approach the hacienda.
Our throats are parched. Our horses are all in.
A man steps from the shadow of a verandah.
Surprisingly, he welcomes us and invites us to stay
for as long as we need to recover
from the effects of our terrible journey.
I lean forward in my saddle for a better look.
I *know* this guy. I've seen him before
in movies ranging from *Attack of the Robots*
to *That Obscure Object of Desire*.
Say, I blurt out, aren't you the legendary
Spanish film actor Fernando Rey?
Maybe I am, he offers, but around here they call me
the biggest cattle baron in the territory.
As for my unfortunate wife, Doña Inez,
she should be very young, but—he shows us
his empty hands—she suffers from an ailment
that is causing her to age at unnatural speed. Dinner
will be served at nine o'clock.
The sun is setting as we return from our
bunkhouse quarters near the stables, sheer luxury
to anyone who has just experienced
the infernal no man's land of the Sonora.
Nighthawks cry from the nearby cottonwoods.
After sitting us down at a long oak table
whose uneven surface indicates generations
of use, our host starts talking about Spanish
poetry, and the price of beef. We drink wine, cut into thick steaks
with heavy, bone-handled knives. The candle flames bend and waver.
I can almost believe a spirit is seeking us.

Don Fernando looks up. We follow his gaze.
A woman in a black dress, her face cowled by a black mantilla,
is standing in front of the nearest of many
floor-to-ceiling windows that fitfully contain our images.
As she slowly approaches, everyone stops talking,
but I'm not really afraid when she sits down
beside me. Could she be, I wonder, a girl
some sort of magic has disguised
as this old woman? She's whispering
to a servant who's trying to listen when
Don Fernando puts down his glass and declares
he has important business to finish with his guests.
She looks at him, not like a somnambulist,
but sharply, as if making up her mind.
Somehow she's standing exactly where she stood
when we first noticed her. She opens a door,
waves her hand, and then
isn't there. Don Fernando lurches
to his feet, toppling his chair. He seizes
one of the many hunting rifles exhibited
like trophies on the wall behind him—
a Mauser, if I'm not mistaken. Not knowing
what else to do, we follow him
down a long hall onto the verandah,
where he leans into the dark and shouts, *Inez! Inez!*
The night's cold air is sudden and full of stars
that look close enough to be about to fall.
Something comes over us—what else can I say?
If you'd asked me my name just then
I couldn't have told you—and we all join in. Even now,
years later, in the midst of another life,

I can still hear us calling *Inez! Inez!*,
but whether in accusation or appeal
I no longer remember.

3

TISANE

[. . . from the Greek ptisane, *from* ptissein, *to crush]*

The bag puffs up in the cup
as boiling water drills from the kettle's spout
into a sudden somersaulting
of almost invisible dogs chasing their tails,
roiling the pent-up herbs into a dizzy
confusion, an infusion of blurs,
a steamy millrace. Waiting
for the one right moment to suspend
the chemistry, I seem to be looking down
from a greater and greater height,
like a balloonist embarked on one of those
self-indulgent, highly publicized attempts
that always seem to end in a welter of news
reports whose only point in common is
the inhospitable desert of southern Algeria.

STROHEIM

for Miriam Hansen

Erich von Stroheim dressed as a German officer
strode into the kitchen, lit a cigarette,
and vigorously rubbed his gloved hands together.
His monacle flashed. Silvana, the housekeeper, continued
stirring something in a pot on the stove, a frilly apron
protecting the black wool dress she was wearing
in spite of the latest heatwave. Her skinny sheepdog lay
panting in the doorway to the barnyard, wide-eyed,
ready to bolt. I saw what I saw, crouching on the stairs
to the servants' quarters, where I lived
with a tailor's dummy, three cracked mirrors,
and generations of flies. Silvana worked for the Count,
who occupied the villa on the other side of a garden
supposedly inhabited by invisible presences.
I was the intinerant piano teacher or lame dancing-master
he tolerated for the sake of his harebrained daughter.
(He had his reasons. I, of course, had mine.)
From my vantage point I noticed the countryside
dimming under a dark, fast-moving cloud, while Erich
von Stroheim, his grin not quite a grin anymore,
began tapping his palm with a riding crop, as if uncertain
whether a war was going on, or just a movie about one—
though at that moment, who could have told the difference?

THE GAS TANK

1

In 1921 the young Max Ernst
encountered one in a dream,
then tried to put it into perspective
by painting "The Elephant of the Celebes."
It looks like a gigantic teapot
crossed with a hand grenade—though later
he would claim the work derived from
a chance meeting with an African cornbin.

Further sightings went unreported until
those visionary photographers of industrial
architecture, Hilla and Bernd
Becher, spotted a particularly robust specimen
in Gelsenkirchen in 1967, shot it
from a safe distance, and entitled the evidence
Gasbehälter (literally, "gas container").

2

It exists in countless versions, round or square,
tall or squat and bulbous, always looking
as if it's not intelligent, holding its breath while waiting
for someone thoughtless enough to wander near.

Its attack—swift and remorseless—features
the use of either a high-powered claw
roughly the size of an upright piano, or a blunt
instrument resembling an inverted tree stump,
the victim being either julienned or pancaked
in less time than it takes to picture the event.

No account describes what happens next.

3

But some observers think they can detect
in its periods of inactivity
a sort of tolerance with respect to dogs,
who, when summer's heat gets really serious,
like to lounge or roll around on their backs
in the cooling air of its immobile shadow.

4

Last week my nervous, headstrong collie approached
the one down by the reservoir.
As soon as she lowered her rump against the foot
of a stanchion, the sound of a distant truck

changing gears, or of my wife rearranging the livingroom
furniture, began to resonate
in the depths of its complicated plumbing.
We both stepped back.

A woodthrush echoed in the maple trees.

SNAPPING TURTLE

You like to lie in shallow, muddy water, only your eyes
and nostrils showing. You eat plants, fish,

birds, small animals. I used to think
you'd as soon bite a broomstick in half

as take off a person's finger. Figment of my childhood
bestiary, down there on the green lawn in the rain,

backing and filling in the wet earth, burying your eggs,
you must weigh at least fifty pounds.

But now, as you sluggishly move off,
trailing behind you in the silvery grass a wake

like the track of a vacuum cleaner in the pile of a rug,
it occurs to me there's nothing clumsy about you.

Sheets of mist shred among the spruce and white pine
at the edge of the woods. Not wanting to,

I see another heavy, carapaced creature, this one
floundering in the fork of a dirt road near the ocean, surrounded

by a bunch of yelling twelve-year-olds
frantically intent on purifying the world

with garden tools and an ax. She can't retreat.
Her blood's as thick and dark as motor oil.

You pause and lift your head, looking around, your face
the face of a hawk crossed with a toad.

Two dogs break eagerly from the trees
followed by someone opening a black umbrella.

LOOKING AT ROUSSEAU'S *SLEEPING GYPSY*

for Anna

A gypsy girl decides to visit her grandmother
on the other side of the desert. Carrying a staff,
a jar of water to quench her thirst, and a lute for music
to keep her company, she travels all day.
It's getting dark when she arrives at an oasis.
After she eats a few dates and drinks some water,
she picks up her lute and sings herself a song.
Then she lies down and quickly falls asleep.
She doesn't see the moon rise, and the stars as well,
and the night turn into an approaching lion.
Lions eat anything from insects to antelopes and giraffes.
This one has to be at least ten feet long from the end of his tail
to the tip of his nose. I can't tell you what he's doing here.
I don't know why he's not back home in some African savannah.
He walks up to the sleeping girl. Maybe she's dreaming about
her grandmother, whom she counts on seeing tomorrow. Maybe not.
The desert is completely silent, except for a jackal barking
faintly and far off. The lion looks around with a shining eye,
and a breeze stirs his yellow mane as it would the curtain
across the window the girl sleeps next to in really hot weather.   ·
No, I don't think the lion is going to eat her. Yes,
you could say she's wearing a brand new dress.

WATCHDOG

Five months old and already a hundred pounds,
head like a cinderblock wrapped in grey velour,
he pinned my arm under his chin on the chair arm
and fixed me with an unblinking, yellow-eyed stare.

I tried to understand, but the heat was something.
The flagstones rippled like linen under water.
Wasps kept dropping stupified from the grapevines.
Not even the chickens were talking.

He sighed and licked his complicated chops.
My eyes kept closing. *Good boy,* I think I said.
That night I heard him barking in the shadows
of the laurel grove, learning his trade.

BLACK ICE

Rain on the two-lane road makes me decide
to give him a lift. The passenger door mirror darkens
momentarily and he gets in, not the eager
wayside youth I pulled over for, but someone else,
pale, jittery eyes, matted hair, teeth missing
in the grin he takes back as fast as he gives it.

He huddles in his soaking overcoat.
How far you going? "As far as it takes." And after a moment,
"Wow," shaking his head. I hope he's referring to
the weather. From the small aluminum suitcase
on his knees comes a cheerful *ding*—the sound
a doorbell makes, or a wind-up kitchen timer.

The dashboard clock says it's already four.
Where you coming from? He lowers his head
and concentrates. "Behind Berlin Mountain. Alone
until *they* arrived." The fuel gauge says I'm down to less than half.
Who's *they*? "The ones who started the war."
I try to see past the wipers into the rain. It's not too late

for black ice on the Mohawk Trail. You never see it.
You only know it by the weightlessness you feel
as the scenery picks up speed or starts to spin.
He turns to stare at the road behind us, then shoots me a look.
"The ordinary angels couldn't pull it off,
so now they're bringing in the *heavy* stuff." He chews his lip

and drums his fingers on the suitcase.
"You got to be one of them."
I've already heard his story—years ago, maybe on
The Outer Limits. Other memories show up as rapid dreams:
Los Angeles reduced to rubble in the original
War of the Worlds. The saucer's ice-bound shadow in *The Thing*.

A deserted cabin lit by a ceiling light.
How old was I when that stuff scared me silly?
Why does it scare me now? Look, I should say,
my name is Jonathan, I'm on my way to Boston.
But he's breathing hard and looking at his hands
as if trying to decide how to use them.

"There!" He gestures at a dense stand of pines
whose tops are hiding in fast-moving mist. "Let me off there!"
Evergreens can have a certain quality in early spring:
a chilly, seductive luster, a gleaming darkness.
That's what he walked toward and where he disappeared
without a single look back over his shoulder.

CERTAIN STORIES

Certain stories live in the air like ancestral spirits
or weather phenomena. You acquire them
from people who spread the word like proselytizers
of the latest true religion. Carried away, ignoring

whoever is urging you to act your age
or at least think of the children, you set out
on a mission to share your inheritance.
But all those talking dogs and kangaroos,

those mothers-in-law and travelling salesmen—how quickly
they tire of the sideshows you keep setting up for them.
How easily they fly the breezy coop of your assumptions.
Before you know it, you're telling the only one you can remember.

And then it's gone, like the rest of them
no more a part of what makes you tick
than last night's automatic drink of water.
The lights are out in a part of you where something

deeper than lethargy or even indifference
has taken over, where your dark and airless fancy
couldn't begin to picture a bowl of soup,
let alone the fly in it feebly signalling for help.

Until, who knows when or why, some eager soul
leans toward you out of the pure, amnesiac blue
and pops the question, *Have you heard this one?*
You don't recognize what he proceeds to tell you,

or the two or three others flashing like dolphins
in its ebullient wake. You're already thinking
you've got this cast of spicy incantations,
as they live and breathe, right where you want them,

they're ready when you are, and they're going to stay
that way—the pig with a wooden leg, the Sicilian hitchhiker,
the Pope and the crossword puzzle, the woman
who walks into a bar with a duck under her arm . . .

LADY WITH WHEELBARROW, OR:
READING A MAIL ORDER CATALOGUE

A tall blond with good bones and a hopeful look
is pushing a wheelbarrow whose gas-filled shock-
absorbers make it a snap to manage her load—a rosemary plant,
some hydrangeas, a fern in a glazed clay pot, and two

heavy-duty garden spades. Next she's walking behind
a space-age version of the traditional lawn mower
featuring imitation leather handle grips and pneumatic tires
on castaluminum ball-bearing wheels that eliminate drag.

And now she's bending toward six easy-to-grow
varieties of lavender bushes that enthusiastically offer
to any dreamer of the country life their purple fans.
Her smile could mean she knows I've got my eye on her.

Sure, she's privileged, but she has a lot to do: pouring sugar
water into her collection of wasp catchers, cork-stopped cruets
no buzzing party-crasher ever left alive;
topping off the glazed ceramic songbird birdbath

that requires being brought indoors when temperatures drop
below freezing; wiping with a damp cloth the dark
windows of the cedar potting shed before changing
by remote control the combination of its Swiss electric lock.

Late in the afternoon, after a dip in the pool, she relaxes
on a rattan chaise longue that gently but firmly recalls
the best days of the British colonial era. Looking carefully,
I can tell she's starting to wonder what might happen once

tonight arrives. But it's hard seeing into the future, even
with a big Mercedes all gassed-up in the driveway,
ready to go. The cops haven't arrived yet to dig up the tulip bed,
a forest fire is still only smoke on the horizon,

and who knows when suspicion will convince her neighbors
she isn't really one of them. So let's not rush things.
The moment needs to last a little longer. After all,
within reach of her slender arm a china serving dish

presents a wedge of cheddar and a single bright green apple.
And two goblets of heat-resistant polycarbonate, the smart
alternative to glass or flimsy plastic, stand at attention
behind a just-opened bottle of Entre-deux-mers.

JOURNEY TO THE LOST CITY

It must have been around four
in the afternoon when the geraniums in a planter by the doorway
began nodding as if listening to a story
they already knew the end of.

I kept looking
at the trim little fishing boats moored out there
in the uneasy light. From where
I sat I could practically touch the red one.

Behind the bar, Max
was rinsing a variety of tumblers and stem-
ware, any one of which could have come
from a table in the local flea market

yesterday or a hundred
years ago. The moment was as good as any.
Hey, Max, I said, trying to ignore a funny
feeling about how things usually

turn out the way they do,
You're a man of the world, somebody who knows the difference between
what people swear they've seen
and only think they have,

or wish they had, or just
dreamed up because they want to. I meant what I said.
Max was cool, unflappable. He stayed
within himself on the job, watching

and listening, not saying much.
He scrutinized the wine glass he was trying to polish,
breathed on it, gave it another magician's flourish
with a small towel, then held it up

to the light. I took his silence as
an invitation. So late last night, I'm standing
in front of the door to my hotel room, minding
my own business, not too much

the worse for anything
I'd been up to, when a woman stumbles out of the gloom
like someone who's just been pushed from
another dimension. She's

pulling herself together,
looking around. I'm trying to make sense of her fatalistic
cheekbones, her big green eyes, the trick
of light that confuses

the color of her hair
with the black crêpe of something between
a nightgown and a Halloween
costume, the spread wings of an exotic bird

not quite covering
her breasts. And then I realize it's the actress Debra
Paget, the Apache princess in *Broken Arrow,* the cobra
cult priestess in *Journey to the Lost City,*

and the first cause of my adolescent
insomnia. Maybe, I think, she'll snap out of it, say
my name, and explain why
it's taken her so long

to track me down. But all she does
is open the door next to mine and close it
behind her—the door of a very shallow broom closet,
as I discover when I pick myself up

and dust myself off. So tell me, was it
really Debra Paget, Max, or just some avatar of the local *zeitgeist*
cunningly disguised
as whatever whoever sees it

wants it to be? Max sighed
and fished another glass from his tub of suds. I wouldn't
call this incident an accident,
he said, but neither should you ask me

to draw you
a diagram. Is inquiry into a dream another dream?
Always the same water, and never the same,
if you know what I mean.

Thanks a lot, I was on
the point of replying, when the room shook
to a peal of thunder I at first mistook
for luggage dropped

down a flight of stairs.
A sheepdog climbed out of an easy chair
and headed in the direction of elsewhere,
not looking back.

Odds and ends of half-forgotten
narrow escapes
started flashing before me like scraps
of grainy archival

newsreel footage—
women in wind-blown dresses squinting up at the sky,
prairies of wheat stretching away
toward towering columns

of smoke, a half-open door
letting sunlight into an empty room. All alone
in a muddy farmyard, a big horse put its head down
and hesitated.

Someone walked in
out of the weather. A double vodka on the rocks, she said,
her glance telling us she would avoid
explaining anything. Rain gleamed in her hair.

Max held up his hand.
The regretful satisfaction
on his face made him look like one of those medieval saints whose
          benediction
always means *I told you so.*

Then he leaned forward
and with a practiced gesture lit her cigarette.
The trees in the window had already started moving this way and that
like an old-time chorus line. Farther off,

a final shaft of sunlight
was traversing the golf course, rapidly
gaining on a tiny running figure who one day,
sooner or later, would be me.

4

NIGHT OF THE DEMON

(Columbia Pictures, 1957)

A strip of paper with words on it
in a dead language jerks from your fingers
as if tied to an invisible string.
It scampers straight into the fire, then
up the chimney in a single ash. And suddenly
who you were isn't who you are.

Yesterday, your god was the scientific method.
Now, you don't have time to even laugh
at anyone who thinks this world is still the one in which
not far from here a tired farmer stables his horses
for the night, children ponder their schoolwork,
a woman dials her sister in Lyme Regis.

Driving too fast through the hopeless dark,
the trees and hedgerows blurred
in their frantic rush away from your destination,
all you can see in your headlights' sickening glare
is that momentary feather of flame,
and the ghost of your own hand grasping at nothing.

THE WINDOW

Uncut for months, the lawn skidded to a stone wall
that separated it from the shore and then
the ocean. Dusk and rain hung in curtains over the harbor.
When the porch door slowly opened and a hush
entered the room with an air of knowing something

I didn't, I wasn't exactly surprised
by the groan of a floorboard, the quick
chime of a cup on a saucer, the soft click
of the latest minute taking its place
in what's over for good. I stepped away from the window,

coolness furling around me as if someone I couldn't see was waving
a hand, or a handkerchief, or a wide-brimmed hat
inches from my face. I caught
snatches of conversation, phrases, epithets,
exclamations—gibberish

about recent events, or ones that hadn't happened
yet, disasters natural and
unnatural, and of course the war. Had there had been
a radio on in the other room, it might have been whispering
tomorrow's headlines. But there was no radio

in the other room—I'd thrown it
from the window just last night. Now
I could see the rain slackening and the field
giving up its last few patches of daylight.
The sun splurged redly. Three or four little clouds

scurried off like children afraid of being
punished for lagging behind. A shadow changed into
a large owl that lifted from a clothesline
pole and with a single wingbeat became a thought
about the dark. Come out, come out, wherever you are, I said

to nothing and no one in particular
and switched on the light in the kitchen. The dog
woke up, thumped her tail, happy to watch me
scratching my head, then saw past me
and got to her feet, listening.

AN INSTANCE OF NECROMANCY

In his Autobiography, Benvenuto Cellini (1500-71) *tells of summoning
demons in the Roman Colosseum with the aid of a priest adept in the black
arts. The next night, in hopes of clearer communication with the underworld,
they return and call up the demons again.*

This time his spells produce
a larger, more unruly crowd from hell.
The priest looks pleased, a little anxious, too.
"Benvenuto," he says, "ask them again."

Cellini repeats his request: Unite me
with Angelica, who's stuck in Sicily
under the watchful eye of her suspicious mother.
Two other friends, plus an innocent

shopboy from his studio brought along
to soften the devils' hearts,
nervously attend to the perfumes
and incense needed to keep the whispering

spirits at a distance. "They're saying,"
the priest explains, "that you'll find yourself
where she is in about a month."
But now things take a nasty turn:

the infernal creatures, far more of them
than the priest had meant to summon,
start to advance, flexing their claws
and stingers, flapping their wings.

Thoroughly spooked, these being
"the most dangerous of all
the denizens of hell," the priest tries
talking to them "softly and gently,"

but he's wasting his breath.
Four "enormous giants" have arrived.
A terrible buzzing racket is getting louder.
The whole Colosseum is bursting into flame.

Showing, in his words, "marvelous
bravery," Cellini rallies his cowering
companions. Then, to their astonishment,
they hear the pealing of matin bells.

As the heights of the famous ruin take shape
in the oncoming dawn, the devils murmurously
disperse, some casting angry backward
glances, others looks that say

they know too well where they are.
Cellini and the rest abandon their smoke pots
and bouquets of magic herbs. Holding on to each other
like schoolchildren, they hurry from the stadium,

already laughing at the risk they've run,
looking forward to breakfast or spending the day
in bed, Cellini, as usual, eager to finish
yet another bauble for the future

to marvel at. His shopboy anxiously
points out that a couple of devils he saw earlier
are traipsing along ahead,
now on rooftops, now on the unswept street.

Which is where Cellini leaves them marooned
on an early morning in 1534,
two imps who could pass for chimney sweeps
standing open-mouthed, amazed

at how the sun flows on stucco and stone, how the air
carries with such tenderness and force
the aroma of baking bread, the yapping of dogs,
the voices of people talking to each other.

KURT SCHWITTERS' REAL NAME

He believed, with Heraclitus,
that the sun is only as big as it seems to be.

—Jean Arp (from his elegy for K.S.)

Kurt Hermann Eduard Karl Julius Schwitters:
"I am a painter, I nail my pictures together."
He loved nonsense, he said, because he felt sorry for it.
After the war, since everything had broken down,

the new could only be created from fragments.
Merz—a syllable that bears repeating until
it starts to mean what it says—rescued
by chance one day in 1919

from a newspaper advertisement
for the Kommerz-und-Privatbank.
The word declaring itself for the first time
like one of the big electric signs flashing

above the seething streets of Hannover or Berlin.
What's left of commerce without community,
an echo of the Roman god of thieves,
four-sevenths of the German word for pain.

Merz, he decided, was his own real name,
and the name for everything he'd go on to make
from scraps of trash and refuse.
But in his *Merzzeichnungen,* or Merz-drawings,

his sketches with wastepaper, he couldn't help portraying
a vista. Take *Merzz 19*—a little
stained-glass window reflecting
the ghost of whoever leans in

for a closer look at a war tax stamp
from a pack of cigarettes, potato ration stamps,
a streetcar ticket, the number 37,
remnants of Saturday

and Sunday, wrapping paper bearing the design
of an impossible labyrinth—everything
in the process of lifting like a flock of pigeons,
slowly, then more urgently,

into a glimpse of rushing cloud and sky.
Aphorisms for the eye
framed in snatches of an exploded grammar
(what other kind was there?)

about not enough food, a ruined currency, crowds
in lines, uncertain destinations,
the indifference of time. And the pale-blue
cutting of an unused registration form

like a premonition
that he himself would eventually become
to all but a few
someone who never existed.

In a photograph his son took in 1947,
he's alone on a distant knoll
in England's Lake District,
brightness and overcast,

water, then hills in the distance.
He always believed in landscape.
He never forgot the line of the horizon.
He hated throwing anything away.

THE HOUSE

One day when I was a kid it occurred to me
that being grown up was what I'd feel like
years later, standing in front of what had once been
my house, watching people I'd never seen before
walking back and forth behind its brightly-lit windows.
I remembered this and forgot it again
as I eased left onto the narrow dirt road
and entered the woods. The trees looked thin,
uncertain in the raw March rain, but the steep,
eroded driveway hadn't changed. I coaxed
the car up it, pulled over, and for a minute
sat there. No lights were on. No one appeared.
I got out, the car door closing behind me
with a faraway thump, and heard the ocean.
The house and I regarded each other.
I had the impression it didn't recognize me.
Or that maybe it was pretending not to.
I walked around it, kicking aside fallen branches,
a few beer cans, a tennis ball, a half-thawed
paperback whose cover was missing.
The kitchen window, grey with salt, looked like
a blind eye, but I pressed my forehead to it anyway.
I could make out a cup and saucer in the sink,
a dishrag draping the faucet, the cheap aluminum
paper towel rack screwed to the underside of a shelf
that disappeared past the pale shade of a table lamp.
Trying the door to make sure it was locked,
I tore my sleeve on an exposed nail. I backed off a little.
Under a sheltering corner of roof, I sat down,
opened my thermos, and poured a cup of coffee. The wind
came and went overhead like the breath of whoever

was standing at the bedside of whoever was
already sleeping. The legs of two white plastic garden chairs
poked from a tangle of spindly rhododendrons.
A crow cawed. Others replied. I had a little more coffee,
then shook what was left of it onto the ground.
My knees ached, my feet felt frozen.
All my senses told me I was coming down with the flu.
But I'd be lying if I said I wasn't enjoying myself.

BACK THEN

The rich wore evening clothes, smiled leaning
against their gleaming touring cars, and lived
in nightclubs full of Latin melodies
I could sometimes pick up on my crystal set.

From its perch on top of the world,
Republic Pictures' version of the Eiffel Tower
constantly emitted little bolts of lightning.
Taller than yesterday, shoulder-padded

women spoke in fluent back-talk
and strode with tipsy determination
from hotel elevators wearing hats
inspired by the shape of a famous volcano.

The absent-minded punished themselves
by smacking their foreheads
with an open palm. Nostalgia was no more
than somebody else's chronic fear of mice.

During long, slow summer afternoons
the western sky depicted in ever more glowing terms
what had to be, according to my father,
the skeleton of an incredibly large fish.

Then the moon, never anything but full,
would emerge from the sea to oversee
a scattering of local small craft
dark against the bright, metallic water.

OFFERING

for J.B.

Some evening, after I've been dead a few years,
when the cabs are busy sideswiping each other in the rain,
just as they're doing right now (a few things won't have changed
that much), maybe I'll be the sensation of a cool hand
on your forehead as you drive across what's left of the Brooklyn Bridge
into Manhattan and look up, suddenly not yourself, at the tall
black monuments stacked this way and that in the sulphurous air.
Or maybe I'll be the radio glow's low-volume sibilance of words
and music you've been hearing but not really listening to, or the surmise
starting to come to you as you take a right onto 6th Avenue, a moment
of silence in the storm carrying headlong more or less everybody
toward the latest spectacles of love and corruption. And yet, and yet—
later that night, for one reason or another maybe you'll think of me
and spill a few willy-nilly drops from your shot of Bushmills onto the floor
in memory of my first steps into eternity.

DESTINATION

How often have you surfaced from sleep not remembering
who you are, or where,
brightness and fog drawing back to show the familiar
still under the spell of the strange?
You think you recognize the birch- and maple-sided path
you're walking on
toward the house whose bony clapboard flank, obscured
by hemlocks, gleams
like approaching water. A picket fence appears
through a tangle of brambles,
and a ladder propped against what looks like a section of roof.
You start to recall
making your way like a fugitive through the winter's latest
attempt at encirclement
and wonder if the footsteps you're hearing on the frozen grass
might be somebody else's.
A quick look over your shoulder shows you no one.
Breathing is simple.
A few leaves fuss in the wind, a branch creaks, a crow
shuffles its feathers.
It crosses your mind that this could be one of those dreams
in which the awareness of
dreaming strengthens the dream instead of wiping it out.
The trees are beginning
to resemble those in a grey-and-white pre-war photograph
on a postcard from France
you stuck in a book you shelved and never managed to reach for again.
The odor of salt-water
and diesel fuel hits you suddenly, like a shot of alcohol. You hear
cutlery on china, people
talking, the waking city's bells like an orchestra tuning up,

so you know it's okay
when you see that the clouds overhead are beyond suggesting
the passage of time.
You quicken your pace. You're there. You're nearly there.

ELSEWHERE

for Stanisław Baranczak

It's almost noon. I put down my book
and look around. A cat stirs in her sleep
on the windowsill, fishermen are passing below on their noisy,

brightly colored boats, one of the two women at a nearby table
laughs, a peach glows
on the plate next to my glass,

and, in spite of the hour, the sound of a trumpet playing
"Stardust" waveringly
makes it all the way over from the other side of the harbor.

NOTES

Cover image: Schwitters made the original collage in 1920, then reworked it in 1939 and added a second phrase to the title: *Picture with Spacial Growth. Picture with 2 Small Dogs.*

"Skills"
Blondin—stage name of Jean-François Gravelet (1824–1897), the legendary tightrope walker and acrobat.

"Mr. Moto's Confession"
Peter Lorre (1904–1964) played Mr. Moto in a series of eight B-films in the late 1930's. Lorre's real name was Laszlo Löwenstein.

"Dinner with Fernando Rey"
Rey (1917–1992) starred in several of Luis Buñuel's best films. According to David Thomson, he was "the bearer of one of the screen's great mustaches" *(The New Biographical Dictionary of Film,* 2002, pps. 730–732).

"Three Historical Moments"
Joan a witch, e.g., Shakespeare, *I Henry VI,* V. v.5.

"Narcissus, Echo"
Ovid, *Metamorphoses,* 3; Francis Bacon, "Narcissus, or Self-Love" *(Essays).*

ACKNOWLEDGMENTS

The London Review of Books: "The End of *Out of the Past,*""Looking at Rousseau's *Sleeping Gypsy,*""An Instance of Necromancy"

The New Republic: "Mr. Moto's Confession"

The New York Review of Books: "Offering," "The Wolf of Gubbio"

Nightsun: "The Supernatural," "Narcissus, Echo"

The Paris Review: "Some Thoughts About World War II Airplanes," "Anxious Dreams"

The Times Literary Supplement: "Elsewhere"

Words for Images: A Gallery of Poems (Yale University Art Gallery/ Yale University Press, 2001): "Kurt Schwitters' Real Name"

"Mr. Moto's Confession" also appeared in *The Best American Poetry 1998* (Scribner)

"The End of *Out of the Past*" also appeared in *The Best American Poetry 2003* (Scribner)

I'm especially grateful to Lawrence Raab, whose canny attention to early versions of many poems in this book made each one he looked at better. And also to William Corbett, Stephen Dunn, and John Skoyles, whose comments, suggestions, and conversation helped at crucial moments. My thanks as well to the MacDowell Colony and the Corporation of Yaddo for time to write some of the poems in this collection.